# LIFTED TO THE CLOUDS

# LIFTED TO THE CLOUDS

Saudi Woman's Story of Spiritual
Awakening and Finding Freedom

HANADI ALMARZOUQ, PH.D

PARTRIDGE

**To order additional copies of this book, contact**
Toll Free 800 101 2657 (Singapore)
Toll Free 1 800 81 7340 (Malaysia)
orders.singapore@partridgepublishing.com

www.partridgepublishing.com/singapore

# CONTENTS

This book is for anyone looking for answers on self-growth, anyone who knows it is deep inside him/her but is waiting for the way to do so. It is never too late to be happy, so why wait any longer? Start creating the life you have always wanted right *now*.

This book is based on a true to life story from one of my clients whose name is withheld to protect the identity.

To my three beautiful angels, Rawan, Rayan, and Yousif. With you in my life, nothing has been the same.

To my teachers and masters who helped me along the way.

# PREFACE

At times we may find ourselves struggling in life or maybe we're just lost or uncertain. Our souls keep looking for answers that are hidden somewhere deep inside our hearts. Some of us reach that "aha" moment, but some of us do not make it.

It is the journey that our souls seek when they choose to take this human experience. To understand this, we need to go through phases until we reach the ultimate understanding of our true existence. This is what I have been through, and yes, I did reach that aha moment.

This is a story of Zainab, a young Saudi woman, mother of three beautiful children, who faced the challenges of life alone. She felt helpless and unsupported, yet she made it, and now people point to her and ask, "How did she do it?"

"After reflecting on my life," she says, "I decided it was time to share the lessons that my soul experienced. It was time to tell everyone, "Yes, you can do it too."

Through this book, I hope to take your heart with me on the journey of my life experiences. How was it, and how did I make it through until the day when I said, "Finally I'm at peace"?

This book is a collection of experiences along my spiritual journey; it is the story of a soul who was lost and waiting for Zainab to find her.

This book is for your heart that is ever growing and looking for ways to ascend in the mysterious universe. This book is a dissertation of a life.

# INTRODUCTION

My name is Zainab, I was the second child of eight born to my parents. As a child, I was independent and did all that I needed to do without anyone asking me to do so. My mom used to say that she never felt it was hard work to raise me. I did what I was supposed to do perfectly.

Ever since I was a little girl, I've known there was something bigger in life that we ultimately all should be doing. I knew that life was not about school, marriage, kids, and work. There is more to it than that—but what is it?

I was a very curious little girl with many unanswered questions in my head. I would ask for answers, and if I didn't get the answers that touched my heart, I would start searching. By the age of ten, I had read many books, some that even adults hadn't read yet. I read books on psychology, human nature, human anatomy and physiology, and even on the universe and its rhythmic harmony. I studied the connection between man and nature and learned that our bodies function in harmony with everything in the universe. That was a lot for a little girl, but it did make my heart sing. I stayed up late just to finish few chapters every night. It's funny that I meditated without knowing that it was called *meditation*.

And on full-moon nights, I took my books outdoors and stared at the moon for hours. What was going on in my head? I was thinking deeply. I often thought of the end of times and how we could prepare ourselves to meet with God.

God was always in my heart. I had many dreams at that age—and even when I was younger—that told me how to connect with God.

This occurred not only in prayer time but as a constant connection with the Creator. Still, I wondered, *How do I keep that?*

Even though many people asked me when I was going to stop, this journey continued, as I had always been in a searching state. By the age of twenty, I had read over a thousand books. I had an unquenchable thirst for knowledge—whenever I "drank," I only wanted more and more.

When I graduated college, the first workshop I attended was on the subconscious mind, and after the first couple of minutes, I knew what I wanted to do in my life. I bought many more books and read day and night. I practiced self-hypnosis, and I meditated for hours in the morning and late at night. I was fond of the silence that I found inside me—that feeling of peace and of truly connecting with God. I felt like I did not belong to this world. I loved my family and friends, but the feeling that there was more to life kept ringing in my head.

Life got harder for me, and my life changed tremendously. I felt lost, and I lost that connection with myself. I went through depression many times after I graduated college. I did continue to search, but this time I was looking to find *me* again.

I attended many workshops on human psychology and the subconscious mind. I read hundreds of books, but I was not happy. Many years passed, during which time I gave birth to three kids. Still, I wondered, *What's next?* I would cry day and night and pray, "Dear God, teach me, as I have spent all of my life learning, but I am not happy." This was my strongest cry for help ever, and I was willing to do whatever it took to change whatever was needed. I just wanted Zainab back—the *me* that I used to know.

Then, I attended the workshop that changed my whole being. I'd told a friend of mine how unhappy I was and that even though I was trying to be happy, I just couldn't be. She told me about a workshop that was to be held in Bahrain, and she encouraged me to use this opportunity. She said that a master was coming to Bahrain to give a Reiki workshop.

"I've heard of Reiki," I said. "It's a healing modality, right?" She nodded, and I said, "Why not?"

I was surprised by what I found at the workshop. For the first time in my life, I saw a teacher who sat quietly and spoke in a voice that made me feel calm and "in the moment" in the class. And then we started the Reiju, which is the Reiki activation exercise. As I sat there, I didn't know what was happening, but something profound was taking place.

I saw my soul telling me what my issues were and what I needed to do to clear them away. I cried in the class as I talked of how I felt and that I was lost. The master touched my heart when he said, "Zainab, you have a big heart—bigger than you think."

My issues were so clear, and I knew exactly what they were. I started to trust more in the universe's messages, and I received those messages for everything that I asked. The true healing began, and in a couple of months my life changed—from the physical to relationships to the spiritual and even to the way I looked. I actually looked ten years younger. People started to ask how I got there and what I'd done. I realized I was being guided to teach people what I had learned in my thirty years of life.

And so, that is exactly what I did.

# 1

# My New Life

I was just like any other mother. I'd wake up early to prepare meals and drop the kids at school. I had plenty of time for myself, but I was tired most of the day. I felt lonely and rejected all of the time. I was trying to be happy—really doing my best to enjoy life—but it wasn't working for me. In whatever I would do, I would always remember my childhood dream—the dream that I never achieved and that left me in sorrow, the dream that was stolen by force against my will.

I had so many dreams as a little kid. One of them was to be a doctor so I could help others. I thought my mission in life was to be a physician. As that dream grew with me, day after day, I worked hard in school and was always an A-student.

I was a quiet kid who respected all people, no matter what. People would insult me, bully me, and even tell lies about me, just to put me down. My only reaction to such abuse was to remember what my parents taught me—forgive and let go. That, however, left me with self-hatred and feeling unworthy in all my relationships. I would seek approval by ignoring my own needs and making humiliating actions as if I was saying: "It's okay as long as you are with me." This eventually led to more self-hatred, as well as resentment toward the people involved.

There were times when I asked God for guidance because I was lost. When I was only thirteen, I felt there was nowhere to go but to God. Whenever I asked my family for help against the bullies, they would refuse to help me, saying they feared a negative reaction. Other times, they would tell me to stand up for my own rights. *A thirteen-year-old should do that?* I wondered. *But, how?* I felt helpless, unwanted, and unsupported.

I was a scared child with so much to deal with alone. No one in my family would listen to my needs or what I had to say. My parents accused me of being a rebel and stubborn, but all I wanted was for someone to listen and help. I was physically beaten until I had nothing else to say. I was ashamed of who I was because I did not understand why I was treated that way. What had I done wrong? I sometimes even wondered if I wasn't really my parents' daughter.

I chose to keep myself at a distance and to think of solutions for my problems by myself, even though this was not easy. Can you imagine a little girl taking care of her own needs? Even when I needed grown-up help, I would find ways to do things for myself so I wouldn't have to ask anyone.

When I was thirteen, there was an incident that I have never told anyone; in fact, I didn't understand it myself until today—I decided to run away from home. Of course, I had no clue where to go, but I was ready to leave the house. As I opened the front door, I saw a light that distracted me from leaving. I spent a short time looking at the light, but it felt like it was hours. I felt something strange that I did not understand.

I thought it was only the lights of the passing cars—and I believed so until today—but how could car headlights be so bright that I could not see anything else? Besides, our house was not on the main road, and no cars passed by there at all; the roads were sandy and difficult to navigate. So it was not what I thought. It was something else. Could it have been the light of my guardians?

This incident is related to one that happened to me when I was nine years old. I saw a light that followed me and told me to do certain things. I was scared, but the voice that came from the light was a friendly voice. "Zainab, please take care of yourself," it said. "Pray on time, and do it sincerely. It is your prayers that you should keep with you." From that day, I made a promise to myself to do what the light told me. I believed that I was blessed to be guided in this clarity of what I needed to do.

Then, life got harder as I focused more on school. I excelled in all subjects, and the other girls would be very jealous; this led to more problems for me. I chose to stay away from everyone. I kept to myself and read books or even meditated, just to feel my own being and not feel rejected and unloved. I gained lots of knowledge on topics that interested me—psychology and the universe.

The years went by, and the feelings of rejection and lack of support grew with me. By the time I was seventeen, I'd received many proposals for marriage. I eventually said yes to a man I had never met—I didn't even know what he looked like. Days would go by without his calling me. When I talked to him about this, he always said he hadn't felt well or that he was busy. Can you imagine two engaged people who do not know each other and have never met?

A couple of weeks later, he said we would get married. I cried and objected—we had agreed to give ourselves a chance to get to know each other before we married. I was not ready yet. My dad was not happy with a long engagement, so you can imagine the pressure I faced on both sides. And so we got married a couple of months later; I was still in high school.

Challenges started immediately, as I was having difficulty studying for my exams, and I was not happy. He was emotionally distant from me. He was either away from home or in his own world at home. What was missing? Wasn't I beautiful enough? Wasn't I fun to be with? Was it just that he liked being with his friends all of the time? Or maybe he just needed time to adjust to our new life. *Well then*, I decided, *I will give him that. He'll change after some time. I know he will.* I was just fooling myself.

There was something that this seventeen-year-old girl did not understand yet.

After graduating high school, it was the time to go to medical school, but my dream of being a physician vanished as soon as my husband said no to my studying medicine. Why? Because he did not want me to interact with other men.

"What?" I said. "I will be a pediatrician. I won't touch men."

He said, "No, no, no, *no!*"

I spent days feeling lost. I didn't know what to do or who I could ask for help. I felt lonelier than ever, with no one to support me and the dream I'd always had. I went to college but had to choose math, physics, or chemistry. I followed my heart and chose physics, as I had no interest in the other subjects.

After a couple of more months, my husband announced that he wanted to become a dad, even though that we had agreed earlier that I would finish at least two years of college and then decide on a family. Again, my life was decided for me. I was killing me with his help and letting all of my dreams and wishes go away.

I was quite eighteen when I gave birth to my beautiful son, Ahmed. It was difficult being a child myself and needing support, yet I was taking care of a baby. My mother helped me a lot. Without her taking care of Ahmed every day I would not have made it to year four in college.

I graduated but felt more lost than ever. All my work in college and being an A-student did not help me to find a job. I kept looking and applying for jobs. But it was no use.

I became depressed and got really sick. My husband was emotionally distant, and I did not feel supported by him. Then I decided to take care of myself and start a photography business. I had no money, so I had to sell the pieces of gold he'd given me when we got married. I told no one I had done so.

I started to feel alive because I was doing something I loved and enjoyed. I became well known in my town and even in other districts in Saudi Arabia as one of the best photographers in the eastern province. After three years, I decided to expand and get a bigger place for my increasing number of clients. I was happy for my success as a photographer, but the dream of being a physician caused sorrow whenever it crossed my mind.

One day a friend told me about a college in another city that gave postgraduate nursing degrees to girls. I thought it was a chance to finally make my dream of helping people come true. Even though I still wouldn't be a physician, at least I would be around people who needed help.

There were many challenges, including traveling to the other city, which was four hours away by car. That meant I would need to leave six-year-old Ahmed behind when I went there to study during the week, only coming home on the weekends. It was a hard decision to make. This also meant I would stop expanding my photography business. Still, I thought the business could wait, but my dream could not.

For the first time in my life, I felt in control of my own decisions. For the first time, I felt free and moving toward achieving a dream. I gained more confidence and was able to express my needs. I was able to say no for the first time too. I did excel in all subjects; I was truly happy to experience this.

A couple of months after I started my postgraduate studies, my husband rented space in a building without telling me and announced, "The place is ready for you to continue your photography studio."

"I'm away all week," I told him, "and I only have the weekends to be with Ahmed. I have no time to work."

He insisted, and I said no, but that did not stop him. He continued all the legal paperwork and got the shop ready. I had no choice. I would be studying all week and then travel home on the weekends, only to be stressed-out and tired after the four-hour drive. Now, I had to train a couple of staff so that when I was gone during the week, someone could take over.

I got so sick that I developed anorexia and anemia as a result. I lost weight to the extent that people didn't recognize me. I also developed irritable bowel syndrome and a gastric ulcer. My schoolwork suffered, and I was tired most of the time. I spent all my nights studying and then crying because of all the stress and no emotional support at all. My husband remained emotionally distant; he did not care if I got stressed or sick. He would only say, "You can do it." And for all my hard work, I did not receive a cent, which made me even more frustrated.

When I read the work for my college courses, I did not understand the words. I would read the pages many times and find no meaning in the words. I truly needed help.

# 2

## CHANGING MY LIFE

By the end of the last year in nursing school, I was depressed to the extent that I decided to isolate myself from everyone, including my husband. I turned my phone off and prayed for guidance. My inner voice kept repeating, *It's time you take care of yourself. You have given people what they need, but you have not given Zainab a thing. Stop that, and look for what you really want.*

What I really wanted was to be a physician, not a nurse. It was hard for me to work for twelve hours a day and then go home tired and exhausted and, above all, unhappy. I knew that I wanted to help people, but something was wrong. Being a nurse is a great thing. I do believe that nurses are angels with big hearts to do all that they do for their patients, but this was too much for me. I needed to take care of me first in order to give to others, but how could I do that? I knew that the issue was in me, not in anything else.

I decided to quit nursing training. I asked everyone not to ask me about my decision, and I did not talk about it either. Still, I felt more depressed than ever, isolated, and lonely. I would cry day and night and got insomnia too. I asked my husband for a divorce—I knew that my marriage was one of the reasons for my pain. I never had emotional support from him. If I cried, he would simply leave the house without trying to find out why I was crying. I decided to stop crying when he was home and act like nothing was wrong.

He refused to divorce me, but he changed for some time; he spent more hours at home. That did not change the fact that I was unhappy.

A few months later, I gave birth to my second child, Zahra. After her arrival, I felt happy and supported by the love of an innocent child. Ahmed was eight years old then. I decided to dedicate my life to my children and give them all the love, support, and understanding they needed.

I devoted my days and nights to them, but I was a lost soul. I asked myself, *Who am I? Why am I here? I am here for a purpose. I was not born to be a stay-at-home mom.* I knew I had a mission, but did not know what it was.

I had high expectations for my kids. One day when Ahmed did not do well in school, I got angry. I was very disappointed and felt as if my head had been hit by a hammer. "After all I've done," I ranted, "after all the sacrifices I've made, I get this!"

I prayed for guidance, and less than half an hour later, a flyer for a workshop was in my hands. I called the number and registered for my first workshop on the subconscious mind.

In the first couple of minutes after the workshop began, a voice in me said, *This is what you've been looking for.* I saw myself teaching people and helping them heal, so I asked myself, *Is this is the dream I've wanted?*

Feeling thrilled and excited, I continued to take one workshop after another. I started changing and healing, which my husband did not like at all. My many physical ailments were healed, but some stayed, and I knew why—it was the marriage. I did not know what to do for this marriage. I went to counseling sessions, but every time I would sit in the waiting area for hours. I never actually made it into a session. I would wait until finally the receptionist would say, "Sorry, but we are closing."

"Then why did you leave me to wait this long?" I'd ask. She would only answer, "I apologize, Zainab."

I called my childhood friend, Hind, but although I wanted to open up for the first time, after all the years of my marriage, I would just say, "I'm fine, Hind. I just wanted to say hi."

Hind did not believe me. "Are you sure?" she asked.

And I said yes. No one knew about my pain except God. And this stayed with me for over fourteen years.

I remember that my mum once told me to never share my marital problems with anyone. She said I should find solutions by myself. When I reflect on this, I see that I tried everything I could. I talked to him. I expressed my needs clearly, and I got nothing in return. I tried to seek professional help but got nothing there as well. What else could I do? I read books and attended workshops on marriage and happiness. I put a lot in our relationship, but the other person was doing nothing to sort things out.

*God, it is only you with me*, I thought. *I'm all by myself.*

# 3

# MOVING TO BAHRAIN

We were living in a rented two-bedroom flat. We searched for a bigger place, but they were so expensive that we could not afford one. My husband convinced me to move to the Kingdom of Bahrain, a small island close to home. The houses there were less expensive, and the education system was much better, as there were international schools available.

It was not an easy decision, but I thought of the kids' education. I did not want them to go through all the challenges that I had been through. I was thinking logically—what did I have in Saudi? Who was there for me when I needed help? No one. The feeling of rejection controlled me to the extent that I thought only of my kids' future.

It was time to sell my studio, a sad day for me, but I was happy that I finally would have a bigger place to live with my kids. After we moved, however, all the stress, pain, and disappointment doubled. Since I was able to drive in Bahrain, I found myself responsible for everything in the house—groceries, household chores, school drop-offs and pickups, and teaching the kids. At the end of the day, I was exhausted, tired, and sad. Again, I had no emotional or family support.

This lasted for a couple of years—until the day when we were on vacation, and I was sitting in a beautiful garden, reading a book. A voice in me said, *Zainab, when are you going to think of yourself? Isn't it time that you stop what you are doing? What are you doing to yourself? Is this doing you any good?* I wondered what I could do to change for the better, and the voice in me responded, *You will know.*

Once I got back home, I decided to get domestic help. Then I started to have some time for rest, but I still was a lost soul. I searched for work, thinking maybe I needed to get busy to let go of the sadness and disappointment. Instead, I felt even worse.

A few months later, I thought maybe having another child would make me happier; maybe the love I needed would be received by a soul that entered my life. I meditated with the intention of knowing what was good for me and what I needed to do to feel happier. I saw a beautiful castle that I wanted to enter with my beautiful kids, Ahmed and Zahra. Their dad wanted to come, but I did not want him. As the four of us walked toward the gate of the castle, I saw a beautiful little boy. He was smiling and said, "Take me. You will be happier." He cried and so did I. I knew that this baby would help me create a change.

I talked to my husband about having one more child, but he refused. I insisted. I felt a soul coming down from the heavens, and I knew that it was my new child's soul, choosing us as parents. I literally felt his soul's presence in the room and then in my body.

# 4

# SPARKS OF CHANGE

I got pregnant, and during this pregnancy I felt different. I found myself asking my husband for my rights as a wife and, above all, as a human being. I asked for the emotional support that I had not received. I asked for the time that he should be spending with me. I asked about the help I needed with the kids and their needs.

He would travel every weekend or come home late, at one or two o'clock in the morning. He never asked about my needs or the kids. I doubt he even knew how old they were.

I felt different, like I'd been in a deep sleep and now was awake. A profound change started to occur. I was so angry and eager to change my life. There was no way I would accept my husband's behavior anymore.

I asked for help, and my life coach, Kecia, said, "Stop putting the blame on you. Start loving yourself."

"Loving myself?" I responded. "What does that even mean?"

I had a dream that told me a lot about where I was going. I dreamed that I was on a train, and as it continued straight down the track, I saw the Archangel Rafael—I recognized him in my heart. He stopped me from going straight and pointed to the right, and that was where the train changed its direction. I woke up to knocking on my bedroom door. I opened the door, but no one was there. Then I heard the angry but loving voice of Archangel Rafael: "What are you doing with your life? Take care of yourself."

I truly needed to hear that to take action to change the course of my life. Strangely, I did not freak out.

# 5

## SELF-LOVE

I started looking for answers and became familiar with the books of Louise L. Hay, a motivational author. I was thrilled to learn new concepts. I started with the book *The Power Is Within You*. It was a simple yet very powerful book. The first page in the book stated, "Who are you? Why are you here? What are your beliefs about life?" That was enough for me to know that the book would change my life. Louise continued: "I believe there is a Power within each of us that can lovingly direct us to our perfect health, perfect relationships, perfect careers, and which can bring us prosperity of every kind." I knew this was true, due to all the studies that I had done on the subconscious mind, but I really didn't know how to regain that power.

I continued until I reached the paragraph that read:

> If we choose to live in the past and rehash all the negative situations and conditions that went on way back when, then we stay stuck where we are. If we make a conscious decision not to be victims of the past and go about creating new lives for ourselves, we are supported by this Power within, and new happier experiences begin to unfold. I don't believe in tow powers. I think there is One Infinite Spirit. It's all too easy to say, "It's the devil," or them. It really is only us, and either we use the power we have wisely or we misuse the power. Do we have the devil in our hearts?

Do we condemn others for being different than we are? What are we choosing?"[1]

Reading this made me realize that my main cause of being unhappy was not my husband or that I did not become a physician. It was my blaming others and always being in the past, remembering all my mistakes and faults and always feeling sorry for myself. I was the victim of my own thoughts. *So what do I do now?* Knowing that made me stronger, and I was relieved that I finally had put my hands on something I could work on. I knew at that moment that my life was changing. I focused more on the inside, and for the first time I did not consider my outer circumstances.

Then I continued reading and learned of the victim mentality that I had—this book was really talking to me, I learned that by being a victim in my life, I was only giving my power away and that's what made me feel helpless. What we all need to do is deciding to take responsibility for our own lives, decisions, thoughts and emotions. By doing this we are claiming our personal power back and we don't waste time blaming a person or an incidence. What if we decided to take these challenges in life as opportunities? What if we used them to change the course of our lives? What if we decided not to be the victim anymore?

I started reflecting on my life. Yes, I had been through hard times and lost a lot. It was due to all that, however, that I came across the workshops I attended. I learned a lot about human beings and how they think and about the subconscious mind. I did four years of *neuro-linguistic programming* (NLP) and did many courses on body talk and many readings, trying to understand myself and finding solutions. It did me good to learn new things and to have new tools to learn from. And in this journey I have met so many people that later became friends.

---

[1]    Louise Hay, *The Power Is Within You* (Carlsbad, CA: Hay House, 1991), 4.

It was only my inner thoughts and how my self-talk was, I was living as the victim all this time and that is why I was in depression and had health issues. I am the one who created this. Now I know this as a fact; time to start changing my reality.

I remember Kecia telling me, "Power is in the words. See how you speak to yourself. What do you say? Remember how your words affect you and your life." Sometimes we do not see how we treat ourselves, but someone who knows us very well—or maybe a counselor or a life coach—might help us see what we don't. I believe we don't see at times because we are just so used to a given situation.

Nicola Cook says in her book *A New You*, "Everybody has a little voice inside their head. In fact we usually have two: a positive, supportive voice and a 'yeah but, no but' negative voice."[2]

Yes, that is true. I did realize and listen to that voice in me—and what a critical voice it was. I discovered that I was always judging myself and putting myself down. I wanted to be perfect in everything, and whenever I made a mistake, I would punish myself, saying that I wasn't good enough or that I was not a good mother.

At first, I just listened to that inner critic. I did not know I was so hard on myself. By listening, I noticed that there was another voice that I barely could hear, a lovely voice, wanting to help me. My inner critic was so loud that I could not hear my inner loving one.

> No mirror can reflect an image of a human, as best as
> his attitude and way of speaking do
>
> —Imam Ali

We tend to listen more to the negative voice as a mechanism to live in our comfort zones; otherwise, we will have to change. That requires courage that not everyone is willing to take. Changing means stepping beyond those boundaries and going into the unknown. We did that on

---

[2] Nicola Cook, *A New You* (Great Britain: Prentice Hall Life, 2009), 78.

our first day at school, the first time we took a dip in a pool with no armbands, on our first day at a new job, and so on. We did it before, so we can do it again.

The words we say to ourselves are so strong that they are linked with strong emotions as well—so how do we change that? Here is the way that I have learned through research and used to heal my thoughts and emotions; first of all, listen and start noticing the way you talk to yourself, and then start changing the words you use. For example, I used to say, "I did not do well today on my exam," and I would keep repeating this in my head, leaving me in a very negative state of mind and ending up disappointed and feeling like a failure. Once I started noticing what the mistake was. Instead of repeating what went wrong. I would come to that point and say, "Zainab, you did very well in your exam. You finished all the questions, did your best, and tried really hard to answer even the most difficult ones. There was one question that gave you difficulty. Zainab, did you know how to answer this? If not, search and ask, and for your next exam, search more resources for your questions and answers so you will be prepared. Overall, Zainab, you did very well, and I am so proud of you!"

Do you see how these words can make you feel? It's like a mother who truly loves her kid, no matter what he or she does. We are still learning in life, just like any little kid. Is this hard to do for yourself?

It is because of the pain I always felt that I met so many people and learned so many new things that helped me along the way. I started to see things from another perspective, so it was not bad at all. Why was I stuck, then, when I had the advantages from what I had been through? It was by changing the words in my head that my thoughts and emotions changed.

A part in me was finally relieved. I truly felt lighter, and a shift in my consciousness was taking place.

Louise Hay explained more on the self-love concept in a chapter that she titled "How to Love Yourself." I really was curious and eager to learn this concept. I felt a lot more empowered as I read further in this book.

I will summarize Hay's concept as follows:

1- Stop criticizing yourself. We spend most of our time criticizing all what we do, think, or dream. We become judgmental of ourselves, but this only leads to stress and anxiety. We need to stop shaming ourselves and build self-worth to have a better life.

2- Stop scaring yourself. We often have thoughts that make our present so scary that we freak ourselves out, while reality is not as we picture it. We keep imagining the worst possible scenarios, and we waste our energy on that.

3- Be gentle, kind, and patient with yourself. We want things to happen instantly. If something doesn't happen as quickly as we desired, we get irritated and are miserable to ourselves and others. We need to be patient and learn lessons as they occur. When you make a mistake, pause for a minute and ask, "What is the lesson I need to learn from this?" Be gentle, accept that you made this mistake, learn, and move on.

4- Be kind to your mind. Making mistakes or having negative thoughts could be used for your own good. Use mistakes in a way that serves you. Do not beat yourself up for them. Stop the punishment, the pain, and the blame and guilt. Just relax, and let go of whatever thoughts are causing tension. Say, "I love you. All is well."

5- Learn to praise yourself. We go through experiences, and at times all we remember is how much we have messed up. Why don't we learn to see the good we have done already? Tell yourself how great you have done so far. Use gentle, encouraging words, such as, "You are wonderful," or "You have done a great job," Even buy yourself presents when you achieve something that makes you feel encouraged and happy.

6- Start supporting yourself. Whenever you need help, just ask for it. Do not let your ego stop you from asking for help. Louise Hay advises to start support groups to help you share your needs and to grow. The love in your heart will attract more people to join.

7- Love your negatives. Accepting that some parts are natural to our creation as humans gives us peace. These negatives are here to teach us lessons. Just listen to them, learn to change them, and use them for your own good in a positive way.

8- Take care of your body. Do not exhaust yourself and work more than your body can take. Eat what is healthy. Exercise. Never abuse any drugs. Learn to deal with your emotions instead of running away from them.

9- Practice mirror work. Look at your eyes and repeat "I love you." Learn to accept how you look and ask, "How can I make it better for you?" Learn to thank yourself every day for whatever you have done, and ask how you can make the best out of every day.

10- Love yourself now. No matter where you are or what your status is at the moment, and no matter how you look, just love yourself right now. Love yourself by acknowledging that you cannot change people, and if not, then learn to move away from whoever is hurting you.

Unconditional love is the solution to all our suffering. Self-love and acceptance are the seed that starts a change in your life for the best.

Louise Hay also talks about healing the inner child. This part was hard for me, as I discovered that my own issues started in childhood. My loved ones have always rejected me. I felt different from everyone else in the family. I was abused, verbally and physically. I was always blamed for things I did not do. "It must have been you who broke that. It must have been you who did this and did that." No matter how much I explained myself, no one ever listened to me. I was always the quiet, polite girl, but I never was praised. I felt that I shamed myself and the family, and guilt grew in me tremendously. Healing that frightened little girl was not as easy as I thought it would be. I needed to "re-parent" her again and give her all that she needed from love and acceptance, and so I did.

One thing I did to heal my inner child was to meditate. I imagined little Zainab, and I started noticing how she felt. Then I reassured her that all was well and that I was there for her. I listened to everything she had to say. She was a frightened little girl. She was so resentful of the times that my dad had beaten her. She was so disappointed when she needed help, but no one showed up. She was very angry that when her older sister harassed her and threw her books in the trash in front of her parents, all they did was turning their backs. She felt vulnerable and unprotected. No wonder she chose to build up her world at such a young age. I decided to give the blame away. I told myself, *My parents did the best they could, and I am now responsible for my own thoughts. The past has ended and cannot hurt me anymore. I need to change my thoughts around it.*

The little girl felt safer, and a part of me was healed. And a new person was born.

I needed to forgive my parents; forgiveness was the key—but how did I forgive them? I started to see things from their perspective. I'm not saying that what they did was right, but I'm taking responsibility for my own thoughts and feelings. They did the best they could, and they had their own issues as well. I needed to sit, listen, watch, and feel every situation that hurt me and replace them with love and understanding.

I made the decision to let go because I wanted to be at peace. I extracted lessons from what I went through. I learned to be more loving to my kids and never, ever abuse them in any way. I know how their future will be shaped upon this. I have learned to respect others' needs. I have, most of all, learned compassion toward people I deal with and understand their pain.

Forgiveness is really learning to surrender and letting that victim child be released. It is about having a stronger version of your inner child by accepting all that happened and moving on.

# 6

# MY MARRIAGE

It was time that I let go of all the resentment and really start loving my husband unconditionally. When I did so, I knew it was time to let go of the relationship. By holding on to my marriage, I was only hurting myself, and I could not do that anymore to the Zainab I finally started loving unconditionally.

My husband was unhappy with my change, so I said, "I cannot live like this anymore. Either we seek help, or we are done."

"Either you accept me like this," he retorted, "or leave. You are for the kids. You are meant to be a housewife—nothing more. Why do you want more? I gave you a house, a car, clothes to wear, and food to eat. Is there anything that you don't have?"

"Yes," I replied, "I don't have a partner to share my life."

He said, "I want to live my life. You can leave if you don't like this."

"I will leave," I told him.

As soon as I opened the door, he stopped me, saying, "I will leave."

I was shocked that he did not even try to save our marriage. I did my best to save the marriage all these years, and the first time I asked for his help, this was how he replied.

Again, I asked God for guidance. I was angry and resentful for all the years I'd spent in this marriage. I asked God to open my heart and soul to see the truth of who my husband was. And then I learned something that really broke me into a million pieces—he was cheating on me. I almost died of shock when I knew she was a married woman.

How had I not seen this? It was obvious. Was I so naïve? Maybe I trusted him, or maybe I was blind.

I saw his messages to her; he actually spoke nicely to her. He took her on trips and did so much for her that he did not do for me. I discovered that I actually was the "other woman." My heart was broken, and when he left the house, I had so many unanswered questions. Why? What did I do wrong? Didn't he like the way I looked? Or maybe I was not beautiful enough.

Why? Why? Why? I took very good care of him and the house. I cooked the meals he loved. I cleaned the house. I looked beautiful all the time. I took care of the kids and their school. I raised them to respect him and love him. He was the *king* in our lives. Can the king just leave his kingdom and move away?

Wait a minute—I was not the queen, was I? I was only a servant. Now I saw why he left me. I had left Zainab before he did. I left her when I said yes to everything he chose for her without her consent. I left her in sorrow. I did this to Zainab.

I was four months pregnant and confused. My heart was sure that divorce was the next step. Fear of the unknown, plus a new baby, left me ungrounded most of the time. I was hospitalized because I had contractions but no signs of delivery yet. I passed nine months of pregnancy and went into the tenth. Six months had passed since the separation. More pain was in my heart. *Oh, my husband, I truly loved you. I was always sincere and faithful to you by every cell in me, and now you don't even ask about me or the kids.*

By this time he was away on a trip with his mistress, and I was in the hospital alone, praying that I would have a healthy baby after going through so much pain in my heart and my whole being. And I did. I gave birth to a very healthy baby boy, who chose his name when I was three weeks pregnant—Ali.

I looked in his eyes and asked, "Can we do it without him?"

He replied, "*Yes, Mummy, we can. We can do it without him. We always have.*"

It is time to let go, time to heal and move on..

Detachment is not that you should own nothing, but
that nothing should own you.

—Imam Ali

So it was. I left the house with my three kids, thinking that he
would feel sorry for his loss and think of the little baby. But he did
not. I asked for divorce, but I did not insist on getting it till the day
that out of nowhere, his mistress passed by me in a shopping mall and
I had recognized her. "Are you Fatima?" I said, she replied "Yes! Who
are you?"... I laughed really, because I felt so sorry for how miserable she
looked, I imagined her to be a very vibrant attractive woman. "You home
wrecker" I said. In less than a second, she attacked me and started kicking
and beating me. Next day, I got a call from the local police saying that I
needed to visit them. I knew this was going to happen, but what I didn't
expect was that she accused me of having an affair with her husband! Her
husband knew that she was in an affair with my husband, so she chose
to attack me before I do. "She was just making all this up," I said to the
police officer, "and I demand evidence for what she is claiming". I never
heard back from the police again, and the case was closed.

My husband believed that I did have an affair with her husband. This
really broke me and I have never insisted on having divorce as I have done
this time. I could not live with a person who knew me for fifteen years
and believes a woman who cheats on her husband! I did get the divorce
three months after moving out, which is only after a few days from the
police incidence. I was left shattered in pieces of confusion. I felt rejected,
unwanted, and unloved. I spent days and nights like a dead body. I forgot
about meals and sleep. My parents did not agree about the divorce, so
they stopped calling or answering my calls. I had absolutely no one to talk
to except my childhood friend, Hind. She stood by my side and did not
stop listening to me. She cried when I did, and she prayed day and night
for me. She was in Saudi but was in Bahrain with her heart and soul. My
life coach, Kecia, whom I called Mum, did not stop calling me or asking
about me. She went back to the United States, but kept contacting me
until the time that she was sure that I was doing well.

# 7

# HARD WORK

I spent every single day doing meditation and self-hypnosis to find a way to leave the pain behind. It was temporary, but it did help me to be "in the now." The pain was hard to take, so I asked again, "God, what is it that I need to do to be saved?"

The answer was so clear: "Zainab, it is time that you truly love yourself. It is time to forgive yourself for all that has happened. Zainab, accept yourself as you are." That message touched my heart deeply, and I decided to search more about self-love and acceptance, reading over sixty books on those topics. I started applying what I'd read and felt more in the now. My days started to flourish. I felt more present for myself and the kids, although it took me about a year. I isolated myself so I could claim myself back and pull myself together again. It was not an easy period. I got gray hair and lost a lot of weight.

I learned to live in the now by accepting what happened, forgiving myself and others, and dealing with things as they arrived, one day at a time. As time passed, I started to heal. There was a spark in my eyes that everyone noticed. "Wow. Zainab," they would say, "what is that glow? Is it a new cream? Or is it a new love?"

Oh, yes. It was a new love—to *me*.

I continued to search for ways to heal, and I knew the mistake I'd made was putting myself behind and putting everyone and their needs first. So I needed to learn how to put myself first without being selfish. I came across the book *Choosing Me before We* by Christine Arylo.

As I was reading this book, I discovered a whole new world that I never knew existed—the world of loving myself and being first in my life. How could this ever be possible—to be me and to achieve all my dreams, yet be a wonderful, happy mother and partner?

Arylo states in her book,

> Let's face it. Not a person walking this earth is perfect. In fact, perfection is an unattainable and rather ridiculous goal. Imagine how much trouble we'd avoid if we could just surrender to our imperfection and let everyone else off the hook too, especially our mates. This would free us up to focus on the only part of the equation under our control- Me. All our relationships begin with ME.
>
> Leaving us with three options:
> Option 1: unhealthy ME + unhealthy HE= unhealthy WE
> Option 2: healthy ME + unhealthy HE= still an unhealthy WE
> Option 3: healthy ME +healthy HE= finally, a healthy WE
>
> How "healthy" are you? And I'm not referring to your physical shape. Healthiness, in this context, isn't about a good heart rate, an impressive resume, a stable financial portfolio, or doing the "right" things. It isn't about eating good food, practicing yoga, or completing a few rounds of therapy. While all these things contribute to a healthier and more complete you, I'm talking about real, solid emotional, mental, and spiritual health, the kind that comes from deep acceptance of and connection to your truest self. I'm speaking of the kind of sovereignty you carry in your core, always knowing that you are enough, with or

without a man, exactly as you are right now. It is the deep belief inside your soul that you are whole and complete in and of yourself."[3]

I did not understand this. *How can I be enough? Aren't we supposed to always be with someone to feel complete? Am I truly enough?* That was not how I perceived life. It was hard to believe this at first, and I needed to finish reading this book and apply some of the principles to myself. Reflection on my life took lots of effort due to the denial I was in.

We women have always been taught to obey the husband, no matter what, and to put ourselves behind and make sacrifices in order to have not only a happy relationship but a happy husband.

Now, how could I reprogram myself to change that? As I continued reading Arylo's book, it really started making more sense to me. "Do I really know who I am and what I want?"[4]. This was interesting, as I really did not know who I was or what I wanted.

Let me see—I might have answers to my lifelong questions. Arylo talked about knowing the self, respecting and loving it as it is, as the key to happy relationships. How could a woman who is lost, and unclear, make a lifelong commitment?. This is a dream of every little girl that later on becomes a goal and, for some, obsessions.

I truly did not know what I wanted and was lost, even though I'd had so many dreams. I just was not able to make any of them come true—and that was devastating. What if I truly knew what I wanted? How could I make it true? I'd tried before but none of it worked, and I ended up even more depressed and self-blaming than ever. I discovered that I did not know Zainab well. I did not give her a chance to show me who she really was. I only judged her and blamed her all the time

3  Christine Arylo, *Choosing Me before We* (Novato, California: New World Library, 2009), 15.
4  Arylo, *Choosing Me before We*, 26.

for any small mistake she made. She chose to hide because of my way of treating her.

*Oh, my poor little girl Zainab. You are only scared because I did not treat you well.* This left me with sadness, but as I recognized that I was the one who had caused this, I began to see more clearly. I decided to heal Zainab, no matter what. The way I talked to myself started changing: "You are safe, Zainab. I just need to understand you more."

As I continued reading in this book, I knew that I needed more self-understanding. I knew that there is more to know about Zainab. In this book, Arylo had stated some questions that help in doing so. These questions are considered a starting point to have the life you have ever wanted.

Let's take a look at Arylo's very helpful list of questions that she posed for a better understanding of oneself:

Lights ME Up:

- What five words describe you best? What five words describe you least?
- What is unique about you? What are your gifts and strengths? Think about the compliments you get from others, or what often people come to you for.
- What is most important to you? Remember times in your life when you were happiest. What did you have in your life—freedom, connection, truth, adventure, learning—that contributed to your happiness?
- What motivates you today? What would you like to motivate you? Notice the gap between the two. What is healthy and unhealthy about these motivations?
- In order to know yourself better, what are three things you can do?

Keeps ME Dark:

- When have you been most afraid in your life? What was going on that made you afraid? What effects do those fearful experiences still have on you today?
- Which of your habits and choices are destructive? Think about things that make you feel good in the moment but then leave you feeling bad afterward. Name three of your worst choices, current or past. Why did you make those choices, and what impact do they have on you today?
- What choices have you made to gain more security – have you stayed in relationships or jobs longer than you wanted to, chosen comfort over perceived risk, or become scared about money? What fears were these choices based on?
- How have you let your choices be influenced by societal or familial standards or expectations?
- What pressure do you put on yourself to be on some certain life stage by a specific age? When has this related to a healthy goal, and when has it been the result of an unhealthy attachment?
- How and when have you chosen comfort and safety over what you really wanted? What has this cost you? How has it affected your choices in relationships?
- What would you like to do differently?[5]

By answering these questions, you will connect to your deepest self. You might not get answers right away, but by asking them, you will open doorways in your consciousness toward understanding yourself. Answers will show up; you don't need to fully comprehend them, but you truly will see the change in you and your life, almost without knowing how you got there.

It doesn't matter how you get there. Just open the gate for more possibilities for yourself and trust the process.

---

[5] Ibid., 32.

These questions helped me to understand myself and to start healing my hurt, lost self on my own. I learned that my whole life had been nothing but what people expected from me. All I was seeking was their approval and not what my heart truly wanted.

Yes, I did need to apply more self-love and self-acceptance concepts to learn more about how to have a healthy life and, more important, a healthy *me*. And so I did. My whole life changed as I finally knew what I wanted, and I discovered the true me who was inside but hidden behind what society wanted.

Now I can say that she is a confident woman, a woman who knows who she was but stopped defining herself by her experiences or even her mistakes.

# 8

# GRIEF OF DIVORCE

So how could I heal Zainab? I felt the death of my old personality. I literally died and was reborn. I have gone through grief for my lost self and the end of my marriage. It was so much to take—remember that I had three kids to take care of, one of whom was my three-month-old baby.

I won't forget what my housekeeper, Suryani, did for me. She was a total stranger who just had started working for me. She was supposed to clean and help me with the household chores. With her big heart, she took care not only of my kids but of me as well. Whenever I cried, she would hold me, pray, and recite whatever she had memorized from the Holy Quran (the Muslim holy book). She asked me to rest, saying she would do everything.

"Madam, please take care of yourself," she said, "and I promise to watch the kids." And so, she did. She gave the kids all the care they needed. She would ask me to eat and made sure I ate all my meals, even though I didn't want to eat anything. This woman, who had lived with us for only two months before the separation, had so much love for us. God had sent her to us. I felt the love of a caring mother. She tried to make me laugh, and she sang and danced.

Oh, Suryani, you made a difference in our lives. She insisted that she stay until I finished my MBA program, even though her contract had ended. She said, "Madam, if I left you, you wouldn't study. How are you going to finish your degree? Don't worry, madam. I will take care of the kids, and you stay in your room and study."

Two weeks after I finished my exams, she flew back to her country. We cried a lot, and she hugged me and said, "I will never forget the pain you went through alone."

God sent her to my family, and when it was time, she left.

In the middle of all this, the pain was so extreme that I needed to seek help, I was lucky that there was a grief recovery workshop in my area. I registered and started the sessions. *The Grief Recovery Handbook*, written by John W. James and Russell Friedman, was used in the process of healing.

Friedman and James state, "Grief is the normal and natural reaction to loss of any kind. Therefore, the feelings you are having are also normal and natural for you. The problem is that we have all been socialized to believe that these feelings are abnormal and unnatural. While grief is normal and natural, and clearly the most powerful of all emotions, it is also the most neglected and misunderstood experience, often by both the grievers and those around them."[6]

Oh, how much these words gave me relief, because everyone was saying that I should not have these emotions and that I should be fine and leave the past behind. How could I do that? I was in so much pain, and I was ashamed, thinking that I was not supposed to have these feelings.

What does recovery from divorce mean? The guidebook discussed claiming your circumstances instead of allowing your circumstances to claim you. How can you see your past with happiness instead of with sorrow and pain? It's accomplished by accepting what happened and moving on in a healthy way. Most likely, unfinished emotions are attached to your finished relationship.

I started applying the process outlined in the book for recovering from the end of a relationship. (This process also can be used after the death of a loved one.). I began by writing down all the incidents or situations from that relationship that hurt me. Everything from the

---

[6] John W. James and Russell Friedman, *The Grief Recovery Handbook* (NY: Collins Living, 2009), 1.

times he chose for me, the times he said no to things that meant a lot to me. I wrote about the times that I felt sad and he left home and did not even bother to comfort me. For the times that he flew away with friends or as I believe girlfriends, and I was home doing everything for the kids. For the times that all what I needed what his heart and nothing more. For the time that I was heartbroken after I discovered his affair, but he escaped away and left me with so many unanswered questions. And what hurt me the most was that he left me to have our baby alone, I was the only woman in the delivery unit with no spouse, this was so hard to let go. What if I died while giving birth? Would he then regret his actions?

I cried, I screamed and chose at times to leave home and go into a deserted area to vent and let all the pain out. I started writing all what I felt in details, all the hurt and expectations and disappointments that I have been through. I wrote and wrote till there was nothing more to add, I felt lighter and started to feel not as resentful as I was at him. I ended every letter by saying "I choose to let go because I love myself, and I forgive you and miss you." Remember those letters were never sent to him, I threw them away and shook off the past away with them.

Great it is to clear your emotions, your mind becomes clearer and you see the truth of what happened. Our minds tend to add a lot to a given situation and causes confusion and pain that at times is not really there.

Writing your thoughts and emotions about what ever happened put them in your consciousness and acknowledging them to help them get cleared from your system.

Some of the unresolved emotions could be expressing your love to the person. How many relationships have ended, leaving someone with remorse for not having said what he or she needed to say? So release and let go.

I felt at peace after that, as I knew what to do with my unresolved emotions. I applied this process in all of my relationships, including my dad, mom, and anybody who had hurt me in the past. I was reborn fresh and light, and I felt my innocence coming back to me. It was a new *me*.

It felt so good to accept those emotions and let them go… but what if *I* was the mistake in the relationship? It was not easy to acknowledge that it is okay to fail in a relationship and move on. How could I accept this as only an experience and leave the shame behind? Of course, I needed to learn more lessons, and one of them is to not take things personally.

In his book *The Four Agreements*, Don Miguel Ruiz states,

> Whatever happens around you, don't take it personally. … If I see you on the street and I say, "Hey, you are stupid," without knowing you, it's not about you; it's about me. If you take it personally, then perhaps you believe you are stupid. Maybe you think to yourself, "How does he know? Is he clairvoyant, or can everybody see how stupid I am?"
>
> You take it personally because you agree with whatever was said as soon as you agree, the poison goes through you, and you are trapped in the dream of hell. What causes you to be trapped is what we call personal importance.
>
> Nothing other people do is because of you. It is because of themselves. All people live in their own dream, in their own mind; they are in a completely different world from the one we live in. When we take something personally, we make the assumption that they know what is in our world, and we try to impose our world on their world.
>
> Even when a situation seems so personal, even if others insult you directly, it has nothing to do with you. What they say, what they do, and the

opinions they give are according to the agreements they have in their own minds. Their point of view comes from all the programming they received during domestication.[7]

Yes, I had a lot to learn, and I—along with that ego that was trying to protect me—had to face many issues. I needed courage to face my issues, to face myself, and to deal with my inner wounds that I had kept over the years. What a journey of self-discovery and self-healing this was. It took me over a year to start my life again and then to start healing other emotions and thoughts as well. I had many challenges along the way; I needed to let go of my resistance to life. I needed to accept reality and learn lessons. Sometimes, what makes the pain even worse is our not allowing that pain to run its course. We want all our days to be perfect, but that is not true for the human experience. We need to surrender to the *now*.

God revealed to David, peace be upon him, "Hey, David, you want and I want, but be only what I want. If you surrender to what I want, I will give you what you want and more until you're satisfied; if you do not surrender, I will exhaust you in what you want. Then it is only what I want."

Trust me; when I made that decision to surrender, I met that darkness deep inside me, and I insisted I face it—and that's when the true healing began.

---

[7] Don Miguel Ruiz, *The Four Agreements* (California: Amber-Allen, 1997), 48–49.

# 9

# HELPING OTHERS TO
# HELP THEMSELVES

Years went by, and I grew stronger and wiser. Then I got an inspiration: *Isn't it time that you share what you have learned with people? How many women out there need your help?* I did not know where to start, but the intention was there.

I started socializing again, and people started approaching me whenever they had challenges in their lives. I realized the wisdom that God gave me when people I did not know started calling me. I knew it was time to consider giving people who needed help some guidance from what life had taught me. I set the intention, and in three weeks' time, I opened up my healing and life coaching office.

I had done a couple of life coaching workshops earlier, at the time my depression. I had done four years of neuro-linguistic programming, had a degree in education, and had attended many workshops on psychology and energy healing. It was all planned from the beginning; this was meant to be. It was like God was preparing me for the time when I had no one and nothing to hold on to. And it helped me a lot. I had all the resources in me, waiting for the time to use them.

At this time I had a dream of one of my masters telling me these words "Zainab, dedication to your work!!" he repeated it three times. I woke up and saw lights surrounding me in my room and they were so bright to the extent that I thought it was daytime. A few seconds later, the lights were gone, but not the words of my master.

It was a success. Many people heard of me by word of mouth, and I started to feel the fruits of all the years of pain. My clients increased over time, and people came to know me as the strong woman who fought for her rights and won.

Regaining my power gave me the strength to go back to school. As I mentioned earlier, I'd isolated myself for a year and stopped halfway through my master's degree program. A few months after opening my office, I decided that it was time to finish my degree, and I did. I excelled and was so proud.

Still, I had questions about Reiki: how did Reiki change me? What did it actually do? I knew it was due to my deep desire to heal and change my life, but why hadn't anything I'd learned over the years changed me as profoundly as this change occurred?

I was determined to know exactly what happens in a Reiki workshop. I found many books on the energy system of the body and how it affects our psyches and health. I then understood that the other workshops and courses I studied only worked on the mind and emotions; they didn't heal the traumas and deep blockages in my system.

I started working on my bachelor's degree in metaphysical sciences even before finishing my MBA and eventually went on to a PhD in metaphysical sciences. In this journey, I understood the human psychology—and understood myself even more, I had more compassion toward myself, and the healing never stopped there.

What follows is some of what I learned through my research:

The body has energy centers that take the energy life force—*chi* or *prana* or *ki*—and distribute it all around it. When there is a trauma or core issues—trapped emotions in the energy body—this causes the life force to be stopped or faced by a blockage. Then that area doesn't get enough ki to allow it to function normally. Eventually, this causes physical illnesses, and many emotional and mental issues are involved.

Stephen H. Barrett includes the following information in his book, *CHIOS Energy Healing*:

Blocked chakras usually coincide with certain psychological core issues- with certain existential biases that your patient has adopted in his or her relationship to reality. These existential biases inhibit the wider range of self-awareness and action available to your patient, restricting it to a limited range of expression. Often they are tied to the emotions, although the mental and spiritual aspects of the being are invariably involved (and often relationships with other persons). The entire life process of your patient becomes restricted. Because the operation of the chakra is so central to the healthy functioning of the entire being it is very important to be aware of and correct any defective conditions in them. Unblocking chakras, in concert with other techniques, often provides a great deal of emotional, mental and spiritual clearing for your patient, and prevents physical diseases, too.[8]

This is what happened with me. I had studied psychology and parapsychology too, but there were areas that I still had no clue about. I applied the techniques on how to change my thoughts and deal with my emotions, but there was a deep part in me that I did not understand. I once told one of my masters that I saw a void in my chest that was black in color. Sometimes pain came with it, and I didn't understand what it was. The master told me, "Zainab, this is due to many issues you had in your life." I asked him what I could do with it, and he replied, "You will find your way."

Reiki worked so deeply in me that I was lifted to the clouds, these clouds move away from my sight—and I saw my issues very clearly, and I started to heal immediately afterward. What I did not understand my entire life changed on the first day of the Jikiden Reiki workshop.

---

[8]  Stephen H. Barrett, *CHIOS Energy Healing, Powerful New Techniques for Healing the Human Energy Field* (New Time Press, 2012), 43.

So what is health? How can a human being truly be healed?. This is what Deb Shapiro answers in her book, *Your Body Speaks Your Mind.*

> There is an important distinction to be made between curing and healing. To cure is to fix a particular part. Western medicine is particularly good at doing this, offering drugs and surgery so that disease, illness, or physical problems can be suppressed, eliminated, or removed. It plays a vital role in alleviating suffering. It is superb at saving lives and applying both curative and palliative aid. This is absolutely invaluable, and most of us avail ourselves of the tools of western medicine at one time or another. However, the World Health Organization defines health as complete physical, mental, and social well-being, which implies a much more inclusive state of wellness beyond simply being cured of a symptom or illness.
>
> This is where we enter the realm of healing. If you only look at what is wrong and try to get rid of it, you are ignoring the original cause of the illness, why is it there, what it can teach you, and how it is of benefit.[9]

Shapiro continues to discuss healing by affirming that healing is a choice to work on your issues, the challenge to change whatever is needed to be changed. It is realizing that your body is talking to you through these symptoms that are underlying imbalanced or traumatized energies. When you let go of that resistance to the flow of life and break down those barriers of self-protection, it is when you recognize your way of thinking and behavioral patterns. Healing begins when you stop the control over your suppressed emotions, it is by stopping what puts you behind everyone else in your life. It is when

---

[9]    Deb Shapiro, *Your Body Speaks Your Mind* (Canada: Sounds True, 2006), 87.

you start focusing more on the inside and have some time for yourself in that busy day of yours. Breath, breath and breath all that in!

This is so true. I was literally filling every hour of my day and night with things to do, just so I wouldn't have to face that part of me. I kept it safely hidden, with no time to reflect on it or even see it. I said I wanted to change, but it was not a true call. When I decided to change, that was the only time I stopped resisting my feelings. It was hard to face my mind, but I was determined. I meditated for hours, just to see what my mind was hiding and to let it finally calm down.

My body was holding on to traumas and negative energies from my past experiences, and I was keeping them tight, just as a way of not being responsible for my own reality. I had to be responsible and take charge of my life; I had to start somewhere, and I did.

I used the science of "body barometer" to understand all my symptoms. Our bodies truly talk; it is no coincidence that when you worry about something, you have difficulty breathing or maybe a cold hits your chest. It's not a chance that you broke your leg when you felt lost after losing a dear one or maybe a job. Your soul is talking to you through your body. Can you just listen?

I use this system in every session I give. This tool helps me to understand my deepest thoughts and those of my clients too. In order for those deeply buried emotions to surface, I needed to listen. Then I followed the healing method found in a book written by Lise Bourbeau, *Your Body's Telling You: Love Yourself.* Bourbeau says,

> The only path to complete and permanent healing is through self-forgiveness. This is the only step powerful enough to let go of your illness on every level, as it addresses not only your self-love but also the very heart and blood in your physical body. As you become reacquainted with this profound love, your blood stream is recharged and revitalized, bringing new life on a sub-molecular level. As it soothes the

soul, so it acts as a salve on the physical body. Self-forgiveness and self-love have the power to transform your energy field, reharmonizing the body's cells as they move through you. If you find this difficult to believe on an intellectual level, consider what you have to lose and give it a try.[10]

I gave a thought too. I did start loving myself, and a lot changed—and that was only the start. I felt stuck only because the person I needed to forgive first was me. I started to apply the forgiveness method described in Bourbeau's book. I will review the points that come next:

First, you identify the emotions. Allow them to come to the surface and acknowledge them. How do they make you feel? We normally are scared to feel any emotion except happiness, we like to hide them and put a mask of "*I'm fine*" when we are asked about how we felt. Then, decide to take the responsibility for these emotions; there is a reason for them. Start accepting them and accepting the other person or situation, and learn to let go and move on.

Next, forgive yourself; forgive and learn your lesson from whatever has happened. Learn to accept yourself and whatever you have done, said, judged, or criticized. You are only learning in life. You may understand yourself more if you put yourself in another's shoes or even in your own shoes.

For some people, it's hard at first to face self and emotions, but by listening and allowing, things will shift, and true healing will occur. Remember: compassion towards self and others is the key.

> O man the cure of your aliment is within you and you don't know; and your pain is also from you but you don't see. Do you suppose you are only a small entity,

---

[10] Lise Bourbeau, *Your Body's Telling You: Love Yourself, The most complete book on metaphysical causes of illnesses and disease* (Quebec: Editions ETC Inc., 2001), 543.

but within you is enfolded the entire universe. O man, you are a clear book with those letters every invisible thing becomes visible.

—Imam Ali

After the healing starts to occur, what's next? I was so afraid of moving from my comfort zone and finding life again. Life looks scary when a new you and a new life is waiting. I waited so long to change, and I am not going back to where I was, but what is going to happen to me?

I knew that this fear could be good for me. What if I stayed in my fears and did not do a thing to change my life? Will I lose all what I have become? There is no going back and I only needed to take action and move to a new life.

Maybe this is what I needed to do—just jog into the unknown. What would happen to me and my kids? How would we live our daily lives without their dad? I was single again—how could I provide for myself? How could I take care of my new baby alone? These were the questions in my head at that time, and they only made me fearful, but I was determined to get *me* back. I would do it; I could do it.

After all my hard work, after all the years of studying, applying, and healing, I finally started to appreciate life more; I started appreciating my kids more. Everything was in color again, as it had been when I was a little girl. And even better, I forgave my ex-husband for all that he has done, and I felt free again. We shared everything that was best for the kids. They started to see him more often. He cared more, and the bond got even stronger between him and the kids.

I became well known in the Arabian Gulf, and people came to me for sessions and workshops. The dream that I had was true; I am here to help people—and yes, as doctor too.

I have never felt so light and free. I know that I am the wounded healer who survived all the pain, only to have more compassion toward others. Thank you, my Lord, for all the love and guidance. My heart is full of your light.

Now, my life is totally different from what it was five years ago—or even a year ago. After giving up and surrendering to my reality—the fact that I live away from my family—things truly started to change. My family called me more often, and they visited as well. My dad started helping me financially and a lot has changed. The way they treat me changed only after I changed my thoughts about them and let go of the attachment to the outcome. And I truly mean that I surrendered. I let that victim in me die, and a new me was born.

# 10

## PERSONAL RELEVANCE

We leave our souls fragmented in all the life circumstances and traumas that our souls go through. Then, over time, we feel lost or that something is missing. This leaves us with blockages in our *energy body* that reflects on our physical body, mind, and emotions. We might get sick or have certain chronic symptoms as a result. Unless these emotions are healed, our bodies, minds, and hearts will always be imbalanced.

How much do we give our power away to people, circumstances, and traumas and do nothing about it. Why don't we learn to let go, to surrender, to give up all the sorrow and just move on? When are we going to learn to accept what happened and live in the moment?

Isn't it about time to truly forgive ourselves and others? When are we going to listen to what our hearts say? Truly listen without judgment—can we do that? Can we treat our minds with more love? Can we be more understanding to our emotions? Can we just notice that inner voice? Just ask: why are we living in fear? Why do we keep frightening ourselves?

We all have a natural ability to heal and our souls are always talking to us through our bodies and even our daily events. Everything is a reflection of our own inner selves.

Life is beautiful, and it is here for you to enjoy. God never created us to suffer, and we do suffer if we stay away from our true essence. I had it all—a husband, a big house, someone to provide for me, a fancy car, and trips to every fancy destination you could think of—but I wasn't happy. Now I'm single, providing for myself. I live in a small rented place. I don't travel as I used to do and don't spend as much, and I am extremely happy. There are challenges on a daily basis; challenges that will be a story to tell someday. Challenges that are giving me a reason to stay alive and work on every dream that I have, but I am not the victim anymore. I am responsible for my own life and what an extraordinary life it is.

I'm not saying that in order to be happy you have to lose it all. I'm saying that when you are in touch with your heart, life will be much more fulfilling. It is not about how much money you have. It's not about your possessions. It's not about where you go on summer vacation. It's not about your academic degree or your position at work. It's not about whether you are single or in a relationship.

Yes, I did learn this through hard lessons, but it is never too late to change. I found a different world, a world where there is only love and other things come afterward. This world is all about unconditional love. It is all about letting go of the attachments to people, things, or events. It is all about love, and love is God. Happiness is when God is the center of everything you do, say, think, or want.

> When you find whom to love, you found life and
> when the one you found loves you, you owned life.
> —Imam Ali

This is known to us but only revealed to those who seek it.

# BIBLIOGRAPHY

Arylo, Christine. *Choosing Me before We*. Novato, California: New World Library, 2009.

Bourbeau, Lise. *Your Body's Telling You: Love Yourself, The most complete book on metaphysical causes of illnesses and disease*. Quebec: Editions ETC Inc., 2001.

Barrett, Stephen H. *CHIOS Energy Healing, Powerful New Techniques for Healing the Human Energy Field*. New Time Press, 2012.

Cook, Nicola. *A New You*. Great Britain: Pearson, Prentice Hall Life, 2009.

Hay, Louise L. *The Power Is Within You*. Hay House, Inc., 1991.

James, John W. and Russell Friedman, *The Grief Recovery Handbook*. New York: Collins Living, 2009.

Ruiz, Don Miguel. *The Four Agreements*. California: Amber-Allen, 1997.

Shapiro, Deb. *Your Body Speaks Your Mind*. Canada: Sounds True, 2006.

# About the Author

Hanadi AlMarzouq, PhD, is a motivational life coach, metaphysician, and spiritual healer. She continues to search for ways to live a fulfilled and peaceful life and to help others to do so as well. Hanadi has helped hundreds of people around the world with her seminars and group and personal healing sessions. She has conducted many support groups to empower women in the Arabian Gulf, and she developed the healing modality that she calls MetaHealing.

**Hanadi is a certified shihan and master teacher of Reiki and certified life coach. She is a certified human resources trainer, certified trainer of NLP, and certified hypnotherapist.**

Visit her website (www.hanadialmarzouq.com), and follow her on Instagram, Twitter and Facebook (drhanadialmarzouq)

Printed in the United States
By Bookmasters